Unbelievable!
Learn About Misinformation

By Sophia Evans

Illustrated by Michael Magpantay

Library For All Ltd.

Library For All is an Australian not for profit organisation with a mission to make knowledge accessible to all via an innovative digital library solution. Visit us at libraryforall.org

Unbelievable! Learn About Misinformation

First published 2022

Published by Library For All Ltd
Email: info@libraryforall.org
URL: libraryforall.org

This book was made possible by the generous support of the June Canavan Foundation.

Original illustrations by Michael Magpantay

Unbelievable! Learn About Misinformation
Evans, Sophia
ISBN: 978-1-922835-83-3
SKU04091

Unbelievable!
Learn About Misinformation

Heard the news?

My sister and I learn new things every day. We love to listen to stories about things that have happened, or things others have heard about.

Mama tells me a story about one of the ladies at her work getting married and I smile.

Did you know?

'NEWS' IS NOT JUST WHAT WE READ IN THE NEWSPAPER. IT COULD BE ANY STORIES YOU HEAR THROUGHOUT YOUR DAY.

Uncle Joseph tells me a story about a runaway watermelon at the market and I laugh.

My friend tells me a story about an argument she had with a friend at school and I give her a hug.

The newspaper tells us stories about funny, strange AND scary things that are happening in our community.

On the family phone, I see stories about our community. I can also find information about the whole world.

THERE'S SO MUCH INFORMATION HERE!

I FIND INFORMATION ABOUT THE OCEAN, INFORMATION ABOUT FOOD, AND INFORMATION ABOUT HEALTH.

I find information that tells me, ALL people in Papua New Guinea live in a house with a grass thatched roof.

But that makes me wonder, because I know that's not true.

DOES THAT SOUND TRUE?

People in my community have tin roofs...

and when we visit Port Moresby to see my Uncle Joseph, there are concrete buildings that reach taller than trees.

I show my sister the news story that says ALL people in Papua New Guinea live under a grass thatched roof and she laughs. She tells me that it is **'misinformation'** and takes the phone for her turn.

Sometimes, it can be very hard to know if a person, a news story or a social media update is telling the truth.

My sister tells me that the best way to figure it out is to ask yourself lots of questions.

"You need to become a truth investigator!" she says.

Become a truth investigator!

THERE ARE A LOT OF STEPS TO BECOMING A TRUTH INVESTIGATOR.

First, **think about what you already know**.

If you already *know* information about a topic, then you are more likely to spot 'fake news'.

Next, ask yourself: Who made this information and are they reliable?

Reliable information comes from:
The World Health Organization,
The Department of Health, and local hospitals.

Reliable means able to be trusted.
Fake news is information that looks real but is not true.

MAMA IS WALKING BY AND OFFERS HER ADVICE...

Find out what ideas, values, opinions and voices are included.

Is there a bias? How does the new information compare to other things you've read on this topic?

Bias means a prejudice for or against a person or group of people.

Prejudice is where you have a bad opinion of someone without having a reason or experience.

Mama says, "If you are reading and getting angry, then your values are being tested, and the site may not be reliable."

It's all about research.

Uncle Joseph tells us to check when and where information is made. He reminds us of the time my Ba read online that garlic prevents ALL infections. So, we went out and bought a whole basket of garlic! All that happened was we had smelly breath. We looked for more information and found a reliable site that told us there is no evidence that garlic can protect from COVID-19.

FIND OUT WHEN AND WHERE THE INFORMATION CAME FROM.

Ask yourself...

1

When was this news made and how was it shared?

2

If it is just shared on social media it may not be reliable.

3

If the information has been on a website for a long time, it may not be current advice.

Next, you should ask yourself: Who paid for this and **who might make money from it?**

Just because it is on the internet, doesn't mean it is true. Someone might be trying to make money from their social media update or website, which means the information is designed to make them a profit.

IT'S ALSO ABOUT HOW YOU FEEL.

I talk to my friend at school, and we talk about **what effect the information has on us**.

"How does this make you feel?" I ask her.

"If information on social media makes me angry or sad, I talk to my family and we look for bias on the site."

She is a very **critical thinker** and adds, "We also need to think about who might benefit or be harmed by this message."

CRITICAL MEANS TO JUDGE INFORMATION ON WHETHER IT IS TRUE, RELIABLE AND USEFUL.

Fact vs Opinion

My neighbour gives me some good advice. Ask: **Is this fact or opinion? How do I know this is believable and trustworthy?**

A **fact** can be proven in multiple different ways. It is true.

An **opinion** is one person's, or one group's, thought about a thing.

YOUR THOUGHTS ABOUT SOMETHING ARE YOUR OPINIONS, NOT FACTS.

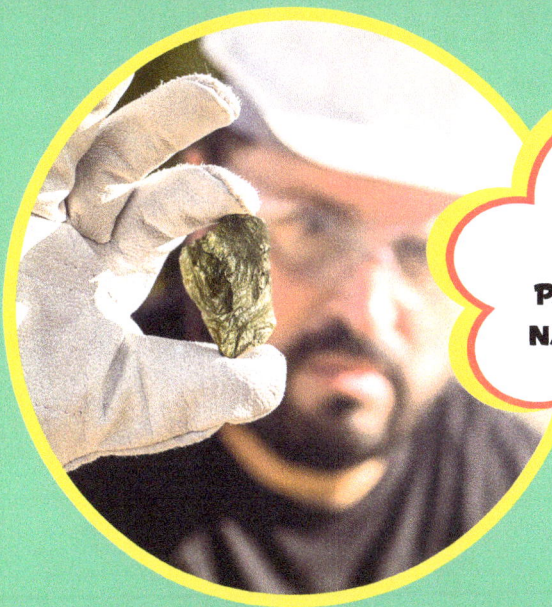

A FACT IS: GOLD IS ONE OF PAPUA NEW GUINEA'S NATURAL RESOURCES.

AN OPINION COULD BE: GOLD IS PRETTY WHEN IT SPARKLES.

Ask lots of questions.

It is always good to talk to your family about what you see on the internet.

Ask lots of questions about what you have read. Become a truth investigator!

When people have the wrong information, they could be spreading harmful advice.

NEVER SHARE MISINFORMATION OR THE WRONG INFORMATION ONLINE.

I look at Mama and ask, "Where did we get the information about garlic anyway? And who did you share it with?"

She says, "One of my friends at work had a neighbour who shared it online, so I shared it too."

Uncle Joseph and I tell Mama that she needs to be more **critical** of information shared online.

She tells us she will talk to her friend too, so they are not sharing misinformation.

My sister and I learn new things every day. We love to listen to stories about things that have happened, or read things online.

But now we are **critical** of what we read online. And we never share **misinformation** or **fake news**.

Glossary:

Misinformation — incorrect or unverified information

Reliable — able to be trusted

Fake news — information that looks real but is not true

Bias — a prejudice for or against a person or group of people

Prejudice — when you have a bad opinion of someone without having a reason or experience

Fact — something that can be proven

Opinion — someone's own thoughts or feelings

Critical thinking — the ability to carefully consider whether something you read or hear is actually true

You can use these questions to talk about this book with your family, friends and teachers.

What did you learn from this book?

Describe this book in one word. Funny? Scary? Colourful? Interesting?

How did this book make you feel when you finished reading it?

What was your favourite part of this book?

About the author

Sophia Evans is an author, a primary school teacher and an avid star gazer. She currently lives in Australia with her giant dog, Leroy. Sophia has always loved writing and reading, and hopes to write many more books in the future. In her spare time she likes to draw, sew and cause mischief at the park with Leroy. Sophia enjoys working with Library For All, as she shares their core belief that everyone, no matter where they are, deserves a good book.

Did you enjoy this book?

We have hundreds more expertly curated original stories to choose from.

We work in partnership with authors, educators, cultural advisors, governments and NGOs to bring the joy of reading to children everywhere.

Did you know?

We create global impact in these fields by embracing the United Nations Sustainable Development Goals.

libraryforall.org

www.ingramcontent.com/pod-product-compliance
Lightning Source LLC
Chambersburg PA
CBHW040316050426

42452CB00018B/2865